RADICAL
HABITS

SADEE WHIP

RADICAL HABITS

DEDICATION

First and foremost this is dedicated to my mom. Always. And to the awake perfection that is in us all.

RADICAL HABITS

CONTENTS

RADICAL HABITS

ACKNOWLEDGMENTS

Being human is the most challenging and rewarding thing I can possibly imagine. Doing it well, with heart and humility and power, makes it incredibly fun. I am profoundly grateful to everyone who has made this journey so difficult and so fulfilling.

Huge thanks to all of my friends – you inspire me daily. And to everyone who proofed this book and gave feedback and enthusiasm – thank you!

Special thanks to Ron Gilchrist for all your support – you have been an incredible friend.

RADICAL HABITS

CULTIVATING RADICAL HABITS

There is a lot of information available to us about consciousness. And many people have dedicated themselves to becoming more conscious.

But how does consciousness actually behave? Day to day, what does consciousness do in us that is different than being not-very-conscious?

Over the years I have had the extreme fortune to engage in deeply honest experiences with hundreds of people dedicated to being more conscious. And the one thing nearly everyone gets snagged on is moving from consciousness *theory* to consciousness *practice*.

It's pretty easy to get, in theory, what

consciousness is, and even to think of oneself as conscious.

But theory can go right out the window when we are stressed or in unfamiliar situations or challenged or tired or angry.

So much of the consciousness that is alive in the world today emphasizes awareness as *thought*.

But it is absolutely crucial that consciousness be embodied – that it be grounded in behaviors and ways of being that are alive in the world.

We need to develop habits of conscious. Habits that are so deeply engrained, that carve such a deep groove in our being, that we default to these behaviors even under the most trying circumstances.

It's easy to be conscious when we are comfortable - practically anyone can do that. But to be conscious anywhere, at any time? That takes practice!

RADICAL HABITS is an insider peek into the reality of consciousness – into what it looks like and acts like. It is not just about how we think, but how we do.

In this book you will find habits not just of the head, but of the heart and of the body.

Consciousness is simply no good if it is a conceptual framework only. You must live it, must breathe life into it. You must open yourself to love and get very, very good at getting out of love's way.

RADICAL HABITS requires courage. Because you are going to do things that show the world that you care – things that will very likely pull you way out of your comfort zone.

The aliveness of these habits can be rather intense. This is because we get so comfortable living in our heads, thinking our thoughts are real, that it is a bit of a shock to actually embody our consciousness in day-to-day behaviors.

UNDERSTANDING THE CHALLENGE OF CONSCIOUSNESS

The patterns you have, the stories you live in, are not some willy-nilly occurrence.

So many people believe that the way to get out of limitation is to change their thoughts. Not so!

You see, each of us creates a story of reality, or what we think is reality, based on actual lived experiences.

In other words, you have *earned* your version of

the world because it is what you learned from the life you've lived.

Think of your beliefs about the world as little and big stones on one side of a scale. Each stone is an experience you have had that says the world is a particular way.

For most of us, the picture of the world we have is not based on a reality of love and kindness and happy people who believe in and support us.

So as we begin to seek consciousness, as we actively set out on a path of greater awareness, it is absolutely crucial that we don't just practice thinking better thoughts.

We must begin to collect new stones, i.e. new experiences, for the other side of the scale!

We must actively seek experiences that reinforce the ideas of love and consciousness.

It is simply not enough to *know* that we are all connected, that people truly want the best for us, that we can express our love anywhere, with anyone. We must actually have experiences that prove this – these are the stones that go on the other side of our scale!

When we get enough of these experiences, this is when our reality shifts, when it becomes nearly effortless to live from the heart, to live as conscious, loving people who are not battling our egos or our fears or our stories.

When the scale tips is different for everyone – because we all have different capacities. But we simply must cultivate experiences that are aligned with consciousness so that consciousness and love outweigh whatever other experiences we have had.

In this way we become able to embody the love that we are.

You can think and contemplate and meditate and philosophize all you want. But until you collect new experiences that counter-balance your old ones, you will continually struggle with the same patterns and challenges.

HOW TO USE THIS BOOK

Resist the urge to read a habit and form an

opinion before you experience it. We do this too much in life and this simply reinforces the old stories. Let yourself experiment and experience so new stones can be added to the other side of the scale.

There are a number of ways you can use this book:

Journal: You will notice that there is a lot of white space in this book. This allows you to take notes, and jot down realizations you have as you engage a radical habit.

Take notes about what you think/fear will happen if you do one of these behaviors then note what actually happens. You will likely be very surprised.

Whatever other ways you like to journal, feel free to do so. Drawing pictures is a great way to go, too!

Divinatory: Close your eyes, take a deep breath, and ask inwardly what radical habit you need right now. Then open the book, see what one you get, and DO IT.

One per week: There are 52 radical habits here. That means you can practice one a week for an entire year.

This is great to do in combination with the

journal practice.

Start a group: RADICAL HABITS are great to do with a group. I recommend you start at the beginning and meet, either in person or virtually, to discuss challenges, changes, and ah ha's.

You can also start a group forum and have ongoing discussion, support, and sharing.

Meditation: There are many ways to meditate – it's not all "emptying the mind". You can meditate on a concept, allowing yourself a very deep level of exploration.

Set aside 10 minutes (or more). Sit someplace quiet where you won't be disturbed. Pick one of the habits that speaks to you. Now repeat the habit in your mind from a place of curiosity. When you get an insight, don't stop there. Ask what else it could mean, how else you might engage, what other insights it can reveal.

Again, I encourage you to write your insights in the journal space provided in this book. See what happens if you meditate on the same habit daily for one week.

However you choose to engage, you will find these habits are "sticky" – they will stick in your mind and begin to inform how you think about and do things.

May this book be a doorway to the wisdom inside of you and support the unfolding of your heart in the world.

RADICAL HABITS

SADEE WHIP

RADICAL HABIT #1

Want the very best for everyone – no matter who it is.

SADEE WHIP

RADICAL HABIT #2

Ask for what you really want and need instead of being manipulative, sneaky, or silent.

RADICAL HABIT #3

Open your mouth and let your heart come out.

SADEE WHIP

RADICAL HABIT #4

Say YES.

SADEE WHIP

RADICAL HABIT #5

Find beauty in everyone you meet.

SADEE WHIP

RADICAL HABIT #6

Let go of controlling and see what happens.

RADICAL HABIT #7

Let people be responsible for their own experience.

SADEE WHIP

RADICAL HABIT #8

Celebrate everyone's success.

RADICAL HABIT #9

Assume the Universe is always supporting you. Always.

RADICAL HABIT #10

Replace knowing with curiosity.

SADEE WHIP

RADICAL HABIT #11

Be where you really are.

RADICAL HABIT #12

Instead of giving your opinion, ask questions.

RADICAL HABIT #13

Assume people know how to live their own lives.

RADICAL HABIT #14

Celebrate yourself
more than you
judge yourself.

RADICAL HABIT #15

Focus on *why* you do above and beyond *what* you do.

SADEE WHIP

RADICAL HABIT #16

Give as much as your heart wants you to.

RADICAL HABIT #17

Be real and see what happens.

SADEE WHIP

RADICAL HABIT #18

Have no idea what someone is about to say.

SADEE WHIP

RADICAL HABIT #19

Stop looking for
how someone
mirrors you and
practice seeing
who they really are.

SADEE WHIP

RADICAL HABIT #20

Celebrate being an animal.

RADICAL HABIT #21

Play with kids like a kid.

RADICAL HABIT #22

Do things because
of how you love,
not because of
how you look.

SADEE WHIP

RADICAL HABIT #23

Assume there is always enough power for everyone. (even at the same time!)

RADICAL HABIT #24

Live like your shine won't burn anyone.

SADEE WHIP

RADICAL HABIT #25

Instead of getting rid of parts of yourself, make space for all of who you are.

SADEE WHIP

RADICAL HABIT #26

Don't take your genes personally.

RADICAL HABIT #27

Assume connection - everywhere, always, with everyone.

RADICAL HABIT #28

Find a new favorite thing every single day.

RADICAL HABIT #29

When you break, break OPEN.

RADICAL HABIT #30

Dare to believe in the magic in and around you.

SADEE WHIP

RADICAL HABIT #31

Trust your passion – follow where it leads.

SADEE WHIP

RADICAL HABIT #32

Notice where in your body you feel truth. Live from this place.

SADEE WHIP

RADICAL HABIT #33

Go into your darkness and find out what's really there.

SADEE WHIP

RADICAL HABIT #34

Shift from either/or to both/and.

SADEE WHIP

RADICAL HABIT #35

Celebrate everyone.

SADEE WHIP

RADICAL HABIT #36

Stop giving advice.

SADEE WHIP

RADICAL HABIT #37

Give thanks for your food and how it got to you, every time you eat, silently or aloud.

SADEE WHIP

RADICAL HABIT #38

Trust people to find their own best way.

RADICAL HABIT #39

Get rid of your rules.

RADICAL HABIT #40

Whenever someone contributes to your growth or your life, acknowledge it, even when it's painful.

RADICAL HABIT #41

Dance/play at least once per week for 10-15 minutes (or more) for the rest of your life.

SADEE WHIP

RADICAL HABIT #42

Decide what you want to see, then look for it everywhere.

RADICAL HABIT #43

Fire your Internal Critic.

SADEE WHIP

RADICAL HABIT #44

Get really, really good at receiving.

SADEE WHIP

RADICAL HABIT #45

Trust that you can't imagine every possible scenario and take the chance on being pleasantly surprised.

SADEE WHIP

RADICAL HABIT #46

Instead of looking for what's wrong, find what is right.

RADICAL HABIT #47

Eat greens at least
twice per day.
(salads, smoothies,
powders, pills,
however)

SADEE WHIP

RADICAL HABIT #48

Design the relationships you want instead of tolerating what doesn't serve love.

SADEE WHIP

RADICAL HABIT #49

Find what's sexy about everyone you meet.

SADEE WHIP

RADICAL HABIT #50

When someone shares something personal with you, ask "What would you like from me right now?"

SADEE WHIP

RADICAL HABIT #51

No one is born with a User Manual - give yourself and others permission to not know.

SADEE WHIP

RADICAL HABIT #52

Instead of pushing, let yourself be pulled and see where it takes you.

BONUS:

RADICAL HABIT #53

Get out of the way of what wants to be in the world through you.

SADEE WHIP

ABOUT THE AUTHOR

Sadee Whip is an internationally published writer, speaker, systems theorist, BodyMind expert, inventor, and teacher. She is positively in love with being alive and has devoted her life to creating ways for humans to have an easier and more effective experience with their time here on this planet.

Visit Sadee: sadeewhip.com

Visit Radical Habits: theradicalhabits.com

Made in the USA
San Bernardino, CA
05 July 2013